TALES OF ADVENTURE AND PERIL:

AN ANTHOLOGY

by

The children at KidzInk

EDITED AND INTRODUCED BY MARIA COSTA
COVER ILLUSTRATED BY BILL McCONKEY

ALSO BY THE CHILDREN AT KIDZINK

THE OLD BOOT: AN ANTHOLOGY

ABOUT THE EDITOR

Maria Costa is a primary-school teacher who left mainstream teaching to create KidzInk Creative Writing in 2017. The reason? She wanted to combine her two great loves: teaching and writing, which is like dipping chocolate in tea (her other two great loves). Maria lives in North London, where she spends most of her days reading, writing, teaching, and watching films.

Copyright @ 2024 by Maria Costa

All rights reserved. No part of this publication may be reproduced, distributed, or transmitted in any way or by any means, including photocopying, recording or other electronic or mechanical methods, without the prior written permission of the publisher, except in the case of brief quotations embodied in critical reviews and certain other non- commercial uses permitted by copyright law.

Printed in the United Kingdom
ISBN: 9798336016949
Imprint: Independently published

For Maya
and all the KidzInk children, past and present

"You can find magic wherever you look. Sit back and relax, all you need is a book!"

– Dr. Seuss

'You can never get a cup of tea large enough or a book long enough to suit me.'

- C.S. Lewis

Tales of Adventure and Peril

Contents and Contributors

Introduction 10

A Tale of Fear (And Facing It) by Noah Bai 12

Trapped by Isla Winter 14

The Wind in The Willows by Aliza Auladin 16

The Busy City by Ahon Banerji 18

The Wind in The Willows by Aidan Lim 20

The Wildfire by Eleanor Ting 21

The Old Smoke by Maryam Ahmad 23

The Wind in The Willows by Clara Huynh 24

The Destructive Wave by Andrew Ng 26

The London Square by Eliyeen Kakakhel 28

The Wind in The Willows by Rian Jigajinni 29

The Hair-Raising Rollercoaster by Avril Luo 30

The Wind in The Willows by Saffiyah Hamid 32

The Flare by Allie Ng 34

The Wind in The Willows by Alisa Alla 36

The Old Smoke by Aanya Shah 38

The Wind in The Willows by Anaya Hussain 39

This is The City by Ella Walder 40

The Wind in The Willows by Avina Sohal 41

KidzInk

A Stormy Slip Away by Misha Wong.. 43

The Wind in The Willows by Ayushi Thanabalan 46

The Furious Fire Alarm by Jason Xu.. 47

The Wind in The Willows by Aaral Bhandari 49

Trapped by Yu Wong...51

The Flare by Aarya Kotecha 53

Acknowledgements.. 55

Introduction

The 25 memoirs, descriptions, and stories that you're about to read all include an element of adventure and peril. You'll meet The Wind in the Willows' Mole - a creature who, mid-cleaning, throws down his brush and scrambles out of his burrow to discover what excitement awaits him above ground. Choosing capers over cleaning? I think we can all relate.

You'll also read tales of trapped hamsters and ingenious children trying to get out of doing yet more homework; fables of fires with twists and turns; memoirs of danger and the confronting of fears. That's not all! There are also descriptions of the city of London, arguably one of the most perilous but adventurous places in the world.

When I was putting these pieces together, I started thinking about the symbiotic link between adventure and peril. Can one exist without the other? Would adventure feel as thrilling if there weren't an element of peril involved? Like the simultaneous scream and laugh when on a rollercoaster, is fear a part of the fun?

Let's go back to a cold January day in 2017, when I taught my first KidzInk class in the back room of a café, to a tiny group of four children. We read a myth aptly entitled *In the Beginning* on rickety tables, and we spoke about words - that was the start of KidzInk's adventure story. Within a few months, I had three classes a week and decided to quit my teaching day job - then came the peril! Would it work out? Could I earn a living from it? So many well-meaning people advised me not to go ahead and to instead stay in the safety of the familiar. I did it anyway because, like Mole, adventure was calling me.

Over the years, more perilous adventures came and went, most notably the pandemic, which resulted in teaching remotely. The adventure to come out of that terrible danger was the chance to teach children from all over the world; in this anthology, you will read pieces from young writers in Hong Kong and Taiwan, as well as the UK.

Was the risk worth taking? Ask yourself this: would Toad steal an unattended car? ABSOLUTELY! The journey that I've been on for the past seven and a half years has been one of the most exhilarating of all, and the anthologies we've created at KidzInk are two of my most treasured mementos from said adventure.

So, to Maryam, Eliyeen, Noah, Isla, Aliza, Ahon, Aidan, Eleanor, Clara, Andrew, Rian, Avril, Saffiyah, Allie, Alisa, Aanya, Ella, Anaya, Avina, Misha, Ayushi, Jason, Aaral, Yu, and Aarya, thank you for coming along for the ride, and for writing such beautiful, well-thought-out, fun stories with me. Thank you for turning up every week, for laughing at my silly jokes and for never tiring of me saying, "Can you replace it with a semi-colon?"

There's something magical about having your own words in print, a piece of your mind and life, published forever for all to see. After all, it's books that offer the biggest and most memorable adventures of them all. So, I urge you to throw down that brush, scrabble out the burrow, and turn to the first page...

A TALE OF FEAR (AND FACING IT)

A memoir by Noah Bai

I still remember that terrifying, panic-inducing, nauseous day – a day etched on my mind like an indelible inscription on a plaque...

It all started on a sweltering June day at school (or, rather, outside of it). I was on a day trip with the rest of my year – 30 or so boys. It was an idyllic morning: the sun seemed to dance on the light foliage, and the lakes around us gleamed like tarnished bronze. We had an entire day of activities ahead of us: archery, fire-starting, and the tallest abseiling tower I'd ever seen.

As soon as we'd managed to cram all the information in our brains like hungry children (which, I guess, we were), the teacher read out the timetable. The first activity up for me was abseiling. No surprise, considering I don't like heights. In my mind, climbing up a thirty-foot wall and essentially jumping off it was, harness or no harness, not the epitome of fun. In fact, it was the complete opposite. Did I mention I hate heights?!

Anyway, as I climbed the spiralling steel stairs, step by step, leading to the platform, I gripped the warm metal railing firmly. All too soon, it was my turn. Anxiety sloshed in my stomach as I clipped the rope onto my harness and turned. I began to lean back, my heart leaping into my chest. Nevertheless, I kept turning...

Whir! Suddenly, the rope went slack, and I fell backwards, liquids rushing to my brain like an undammed river. I was rooted to the spot. Ever so slowly, I placed another foot behind me and eased out the tension on the cord. Voices cheered me on, soothing me like a safety blanket as I lowered myself, inch by inch, towards firm ground.

I now know what they mean by "so close yet so far". Hanging there, suspended barely a metre above the ground, I could've been lightyears away as I took those final steps. With legs of melting butter, I jumped down onto the carpet of bark and pine needles that coated the floor. Triumph flared like a firework on a short fuse, and I finally stretched my shaking arms.

After that day, I learnt that fear is like a spring-loaded gun: if you don't press it down, it will jump back on you when you're not watching. You have to fire it – or face it – before it gets you first. So, if you ask me if I like abseiling, I'll say yes... to everything except those horrible harnesses.

TRAPPED

A story by Isla Winter

Cautiously, I scanned the enclosed, tight, small coach with a tranquil demeanour: infectious joy energised the vehicle like a fizzy drink while the idyllic sky was as clear as crystal. Happy, excited and pleased, the children's faces lit up at the sight of the fun, spectacular, amazing school trip they had experienced – it had been a magnificent day for an adventure.

As I searched the coach for lost belongings, a sudden, peculiar sound could be heard. A shuddering gurgle crowded the air. What was it, snoring? Finally, I spotted a noisy, brown-haired boy sleeping, like a baby cuddling its teddy bear.

"Come on, Jeremy, quick, we are going to be left behind!" I exclaimed, tapping him on the shoulder.

"Wait, what?" Jeremy questioned, perplexed, jolting awake.

"Quick Jeremy, we will get trapped in the coach if we don't escape soon, oh no..." I repeated.

"Oh no what?" Jeremy queried, with shining dazzling eyes as blue as a diamond, wondering to himself what was happening.

Staring into Jeremy's pale, anxious face, I felt a shiver ran down my spine. Oh no...the doors automatically locked us in after ten minutes. What a silly system! With determination, I barged the door combining all my weight on it; it was no use, I hadn't made any effect at all. The lights began to flicker, and we were suddenly plunged into darkness. All I could do was sit down momentarily with a hopeless sigh; we were done for.

As multiple thoughts crossed my mind, I realised this was the coach car park, not for cars, so no teachers would come here unless on another school trip. Sitting down in the corner of the coach, my teeth chattered while tears rolled down my cheeks like rivulets. My jaw fell wide open like a tiger about to eat its prey; my heart pounded like a bass drum; my body froze like a statue.

"Are you claustrophobic?" Jeremy asked, with a twinkle in his eye (he clearly sounded delighted to be braver than me).

"Well, yes -" I began to say.

"Then we must get you out quick!" the young student exclaimed, running around and panning the eerie coach.

"Look, I found a boomerang. I'll throw it at the window, and we can escape! Stand back!" Jeremy bellowed, preparing to hit the glass with all his strength.

Smash! Glass scattered across the scene like jigsaw pieces. Jumping up with joy, I hurriedly exited the coach and thanked Jeremy as much as I could before a sudden, deafening, blaring horn penetrated my ears...

Beep! Ding! My weary eyes opened as slow as a sloth. It was just a dream! Relieved, relaxed and calm, I checked my phone. What had I got on today? The school trip!

"Oh no..." I muttered to myself, pulling the covers over me.

THE WIND IN THE WILLOWS
A continuation by Aliza Auladin

Scampering and scuttling, beaming and grinning, Mole cuddled the incandescent, warm and welcoming rays of the sun, while he blissfully scrambled over the emerald-green hills. The smell of fresh green grass awakened his senses and the lake - glistening and gleaming like a cobalt sapphire - rippled melodiously.

"This is fine!" he said to himself jubilantly.

Despite Mole feeling elated and contented, a sudden darkness started to creep up on him, and a quivering breeze enveloped the air. The sun was now a snuffed-out candle as pewter-grey clouds blocked the golden rays of sunlight which had previously shone down on him. He shuddered under the shadows. It was getting dark. Mole was alone. Mole was scared. Mole was lost...

Whimpering and whinging, muttering and mumbling, the little creature gazed at his unfamiliar surroundings: large, lofty trees loomed above him like great giants, while the clouds were an endless trail of gloom. Splish! Splash! Splosh! Rain fell from the sky in slanted lines, slapping the earth with its wet blows. A wailing wind whipped across Mole, choking and threatening the cold, crisp air.

"This is worse than white-washing!" he exclaimed timorously.

Panting and gasping heavily, he searched for shelter. The rain, which pelted down like bullets, fell harder now, lashing from the blanket of darkness above him. Irritating dust gritted his eyes and tickled the back of his throat; water ran off his soaked black fur, and his aching back and weary arms grew heavy as lead. Alarm set in. Desperately, he scraped and scratched and scabbled and scrounged, trying to find a way out...

THE BUSY CITY

A descriptive piece by Ahon Banerji

Crowded, cramped, and congested are the words that spring to mind as I exit the station and meet with the city of London again. Within a few seconds, I'm drowning in a sea of people on the train platform. Everyone is at the station trying to rush out so that they can catch a bus. Commuters rush to go to their offices: they have to earn money. A person just gets to go out of the long, narrow and iconic vehicle that is starting to move on the thin rail tracks.

Out of the tunnel, the whipping wind bites at my face as specks of rain trickle down my nose. Gazing around in wonder at the feast in front of me, the horns of cars and buses strike my ear drum. Everyone in the packed metropolis is wrapped with energy and cheerfulness, enjoying every moment in the Big Smoke. Citizens of London always have a shopping bag in their hand – it's a shopper's paradise. I wonder what is inside the bags - could it be souvenirs? Or could they be filled with fashionable clothes or exotic showpieces to decorate their homes with? Despite the different choices and movements, there is an inherent joy emanating from the city. Like the cars on the road, the pavement-grey clouds are taking over the sky. Curiosity fizzes through me.

After a few seconds, I turn my attention to the cobbled side roads dotted with numerous cafes. One of these is the popular haunt of three friends discussing the world over a hot cuppa. Children are enjoying their waffles and hot chocolates that make my stomach (which is always hungry) rumble. Raven-black cabs and double-decker cherry-red buses are busy transporting city-dwellers and tourists; the smell of diesel, which wafts up my nose, sadly replaces the delicious scent of waffles as I stroll on.

Like a sponge, I absorb the excitement the city embodies. As I walk and gaze at the towering buildings, my legs elongate and stretch, befriending the pavement beneath them. I then decide to rest at a café by the River Thames. A cup of hot chocolate brings a sense of immense satisfaction.

My city tour has been heart-warming, and I want to return to this charm time and again.

THE WIND IN THE WILLOWS
A continuation piece by Aidan Lim

Skipping and scurrying, beaming and giggling, Mole (who was very lively) pursued his way across the meadow while the birds hummed in the emerald-green trees. The little creature - curious and interested - saw another mole rolling in the warm grass.

"Who is that?" he questioned curiously...

"Hi Mole, do you want to go on the lake in my boat?" said the other mole, who was still rolling in the grass "My name is Molly!"

Ecstatically, Mole sprang off all his four legs at once and exclaimed "Of course!" as a soft breeze caressed his brow.

Like a dart, he skipped into the distance to the boat while the sun beamed down on him.

When they reached their destination, they leaped onto the boat. Instantly, Molly steered the vessel using her paddles. It swerved left and right on the water like a flower swaying in the wind. The breeze - which was like a paintbrush - caressed his brow. Around them, the calm lake was a mirror reflecting light from the sun; they floated across the river.

Mole was relaxing when he heard a crash... Out of the blue, thunder clapped in the air, the clouds raged, the wind howled, the waves bellowed; the mast groaned in agony, fighting the storm, gasping for life.

A thunderstorm was brewing. Splash! A wave hurled Molly off the deck; she screeched in agony. Mole gasped in terror...

THE WILDFIRE

A story by Eleanor Ting

The wildfire was raging. Glowing, flaring and scorching, the remorseless flames gobbled up the town like a famished lion. Smash! A brick fell to the ground as a brown-haired girl wailed from the top floor flat.

"Help me! I feel hot! Please help me!" she shrieked.

Panic-stricken, Ogon was rooted to the ground like a tree, his hands sweating inside his fire gloves. The screaming of the girl faded away: he closed his eyes and remembered the time when his daughter, Millie, stretched out her tender arms begging for another warm hug until the fire took her away. *I miss her terribly,* he thought.

"This one's for Millie," he declared, before a wave of determination swept through him; he left his commander and his fear behind...

Like a fox, Ogon darted through the firestorm and up the stairs.

"Hang on!" he bellowed, nearly choking on fumes, "I am almost there. You'll be okay! You'll be safe, don't panic! I'll be there for you!"

Gently, Ogon scooped the little girl up just like how he used to pick up Millie.

Down the stairs they went, the fireman and the girl, each step harder than the last. Once they exited the blazing building, he passed the little girl to her grateful parents before falling to the ground. Suddenly, all his was anxiety gone. All was silent. Dark...

"Dad, can you give me another hug, please?" pleaded a soft voice. The voice belonged to a girl who is a fan of hugs.

"Millie?" Ogon muttered before he closed his eyes forever.

Ogon: "fire" in Russian
Millie: "cute" in Russian

THE OLD SMOKE
A descriptive piece by Maryam Ahmad

Miserable, thunderous, raging rain strikes my umbrella. Like a warming fire, the cathedral greets me for shelter. People shove me; coats brush past me as their escape from the rain becomes priority. I glance up at the clock across the street, feeling the rhythm of the ticking second hand. Time is racing ahead. Above me, a flock of pigeons fly past (and instinctively I cover my head).

The tenebrific taxis scurry around like mice. Zoom! Rapid cars race through traffic lights as if on a Formula One racing track, all whilst people rush about like ants. A car zips past, splashing a woman rushing to catch the tomato-red bus. She is now wet, and I am dry.

Despite the howling wind, the shoppers continue to rush about. In the background, towering buildings keep their watchful eyes on the city, like a parent with their child. Clouds appear smoky, and frowns appear on the faces of people. I am exhausted. Crowds gather in coffee shops and buildings. All the rush causes a man to trip as if he has slipped on a banana peel.

Within seconds, I taste the salty rain drops that trickle with ease from my forehead, down the bridge of my nose and onto the parting of my lips. This happens the very instant I step forward into the road. What a shame!

Pelt! Pelt! Pelt! I am no longer dry... I am no longer protected... I am, certainly, no longer enjoying the moment...

THE WIND IN THE WILLOWS
A continuation by Clara Huynh

Smiling and scuttering, scurrying and skipping, Mole continued on his adventure before eventually getting tired from running up the steep hill. The little creature - exhausted and tired - lay next to the serene, cerulean and tranquil river.

'This is spectacular!' he exclaimed cheerfully.

After three long, sleepy hours, Mole awoke in the worst way possible: by falling into a river - well nearly falling in, but something grabbed his left hand before he plummeted...

...A Rat!

"Phew, that was very close!" he said with his kind heart beating rapidly.

"Hello, my name is Mole, what is yours?"

"Rat. I just moored my boat to have a picnic here, but as I was setting up you were about to fall," the Water Rat replied.

"Well, that's very kind, thank you."

"I don't have any friends, but would you like to have a picnic with me?" Rat asked hopefully.

"Sure."

One joyous hour later, Mole - considerate and thankful - enjoyed the meal and noticed he had a lot in common with Rat. Mole and Rat were tired and weary, so they slept under the chocolate-brown tree, where they fell asleep after counting all the shimmering stars that shone as brightly as jewellery.

In the morning, Mole was awoken by a large splash of water on him. At first, he was confused, but then he saw Rat on his wooden boat.

"We're going to sail today," said Rat.

"I don't know what you mean, but it sounds like fun," Mole replied cheerfully.

"You don't know about sailing? What kind of prison have you been put in?!"

"What do you mean, I haven't been in prison?" Mole said.

"Anyway, sailing is fun - you go on a boat and ride!" Rat said.

So, off they went... They talked for hours and hours until their stomachs rumbled as loud as lawnmowers. They ate sandwiches and continued to sail. Mole couldn't stop thinking about home. Although he loved the colourful, vivid and bright flowers, and the stars at nighttime, he missed having to deep clean his home every month and the cosy and comfortable furniture. It was clear that Mole was homesick and down in the dumps, but he was pure-hearted and didn't want to leave his new friend without telling him.

After a while, Mole summoned all his courage to tell his dearest friend Rat that he'd have to go back to his home.

"Here goes, " said Mole, "Rat..."

"Yes, Mole?"

"I have to go back to my home because I miss it so much even if it's only been a few days," Mole uttered.

"Wow that's fantastic I could come and live with you if that's okay,"

"That's brilliant, why didn't I think of that?!" Mole exclaimed.

THE DESTRUCTIVE WAVE
A story by Andrew Ng

Blazing, crackling, sizzling, the flames washed over the city like a destructive wave. Boom! The East side of the building fell to the ground with an ear-splitting crack! High above, a baby wrapped in clothes balanced perilously on top of the last single tower of the building. The baby cried and wailed, but there was no one to save him, was there...?

Timorous, Pydrew was rooted to the ground like a tree, his fire coat smothering him like the smoke above him. As the baby's cries mixed with the sound of debris falling from the tower, he closed his eyes and remembered his parents smiling, like the sun on a beach, before the day they died. His blue eyes brimmed with tears, his knees shook like jelly, and he sank to the ground slowly. *I miss them every second of every day*, he thought. He slowly rose, confidence pouring energy into him. A warm feeling spread through his body.

He yelled, "For my parents!" before charging into the fire like a soldier charging into battle...

Like a tsunami, the heat and flames rolled over him, devouring him. Ribbons of fire choked him like a noose, burning him like a furnace. The flames were an impenetrable wall, preventing him from saving the baby at all costs. However, he persevered, never budging, and after what seemed like decades, the flames gave out to him. He leapt with inhuman strength and... saved the baby before the top of the tower broke in half!

With the baby in his arms, he clambered through the wreckage like a monkey, heading straight for the exit. At the last moment, the building groaned, the now half-melted supporting columns gave out, and the building fell over as if it were a shot man. Pydrew ran toward the exit with his remaining strength, and threw the baby to the nearest paramedic, before the exit slammed shut like a jaw, trapping him forever in the building.

The last few seconds Pydrew lived seemed to him like hours. Two warm and inviting hands reached towards him and he saw his parents smiling faces through the smoke, and he heard them say "Good night, Pydrew!"

His vision blurred and everything turned hazy, and as his eyes closed for the last time, there was a happy smile on his face.

THE LONDON SQUARE
A descriptive piece by Eliyeen Kakakhel

As the glitter of the sun diminishes, aged lampposts lead the way for me. London life is still young, far from fading anytime soon. A myriad of people, vehicles and shops fill the streets to the brim. Plip plop. Despite the gushing rain, Londoners are undaunted - everyone does what they must - there is no pause button on this avenue. What a city this is!

I arrive at the square, staring in awe. This bustling, monochromatic gem is protected by a series of skyscrapers that act like guards. I absorb the surroundings. The misty grey sky closes in, but this street is undeterred, bustling as if it were a sunny day. I stand in the middle of the commotion, hundreds of locals and tourists hastily making their way out, tugging at my coat from right and left. I feel an unplaceable feeling that I'm lost - the wave of people know exactly where to go, but I am confused. The square is overwhelming me with its bright neon signs and cramped spaces, so I frantically look around for something comforting.

Just then, the aroma of freshly baked bread and buns fills the air, making my stomach yearn for the carbohydrate goodness. This heavenly scent is followed by wafts of sugary ones blending with cinnamon and dried ginger. Wishing I had some spare change, I drank in the smells, tasting the food in my mind as I walked past along.

As my day trip here comes to a close, my heart longs to visit this beauty once more...

THE WIND IN THE WILLOWS
A continuation by Rian Jigajinni

As the minutes marched on, the two amiable friends alighted the boat while the sun – as yellow as a citrine jewel – shone radiantly on their faces. Well, to Rat, the sun shone radiantly; Mole, however, was thinking of the harrowing, cold moonlit nights in the Wild Woods where the toxic air was aloof. The soft blades of grass (or, from Mole's perspective, penetrating needles) brushed their furry feet as Rat laid down the velvety blanket, soon to be indolently sat on. On the other hand, Mole was hindered by the thought of terrifying, distorted trees with sodden, skeletal limbs...

Finally, Rat finished preparing the picnic and gaudily said, 'Take a gander at my boutique foods: fresh handpicked berries and pigs-in-blankets covered in a pastry adorned with harlequin designs. Beautiful, right?'

'Thank you- it is extremely enticing. Um, what else is in the W-W-Wild wood?' questioned Mole as he bit his nails.

'Oh, you know, blood-thirsty monsters with flesh-ripping teeth and, the cherry on top, an appetite for moles.'

'It can't be true!' cried Mole, terrified, as the whites of his knuckles gripped Rat's arm tightly.

Crack! Mole's knuckles whitened even more. He couldn't hold in the fear. Relinquishing his friend's arm, he ran and screamed through the woods, his tiny hands flailing in the air, his feeble muscles tired of the agonising ache. No balm could soothe Mole's fear. It was a fear that would last for a very long time. The wooded vicinity he was scrambling into, was the very place he had wanted to elude...

THE HAIR-RAISING ROLLERCOASTER

A memoir by Avril Luo

I still remember that horrifying, hair-raising, worrying day - a day that lives in my mind as if it were yesterday...

It all started when my family and I went to Chessington World of Adventures. It was a beautiful day: the sun was as bright as a diamond and the sky was a canvas of blue. Around me, people were screaming with delight, excited children holding candy floss and teenagers queuing for rollercoasters. It was so exciting!

As we stood in the queue to the rollercoaster (called The Intimidator), my stomach fizzed with anxiety like the sizzle of a fried egg on a hot pan; the dark corridor towards the thrill ride felt like it was mocking me, saying: "You're such a coward, you can't do this!"

Nonetheless, I persevered...

Suddenly, the sun became hot and ferocious, burning into my skin. I wiped some sweat off my forehead. The rollercoaster came into view, and I stepped into it. When everybody was strapped in, the ride started. As we ascended the slope, my hands became sweaty, and I gripped the bar tighter. Adrenaline pumped in my veins. All at once, the rollercoaster dropped, but my tummy stayed up in the air before plummeting down again and rejoining me. I squeezed my eyes shut in anxiety as the pull of the big dipper threw me around...

It went on for all eternity! The ride went on and on, as if there was no end. Finally, it slowed down to a tortoise-like pace, and we arrived where we started. With wobbly legs, I climbed off the rollercoaster. I did it! Euphoria spread through me. The sun became cool, and a soft breeze caressed my cheeks.

After that day, I always tried to go on rollercoasters, no matter how scary they looked. After all, you don't know unless you try. My mum and dad had encouraged me to go on the rollercoaster; and then I felt like I wanted to ride on it again and again!

THE WIND IN THE WILLOWS
A continuation by Saffiyah Hamid

Scampering and smiling, beaming and chuckling, Mole embraced the warmth of the welcoming sun; his face creased into a large grin. The curious creature - eager and exhilarated - peered through the viridescent bushes.

"This is better than whitewashing," he exclaimed, heaving a sigh of relief.

A soft breeze caressed his heated brow before he heard a SPLASH...

...It was Water Rat!

"Hello Mole! Would you like to come on my boat on this beautiful day?" asked Ratty, his sleek fur glistening in the golden sun.

With his sapphire eyes dazzling like priceless diamonds dug deep from a mine, Mole nodded. How could he possibly refuse this brilliant opportunity? Cautiously climbing into the small, wooden boat, he admired the wild colours of the delicate, young, vivid flowers that swayed gracefully in the gentle wind. A few moments later, they were exploring areas, previously unknown to Mole: coral-pink and cherry-red roses were blooming out of the ground. Bushes were erupting with lavender. The lake - which was as clear and crisp as a mirror - rippled gently. Bliss hung in the air.

"Can I row please?" Mole asked eagerly.

Reluctantly the Water Rat sighed, and handed over the lightweight, oak oars.

"Just be careful. Do not get distracted by anything," he replied heavily.

For a while, things were going smoothly. However, when curious Mole spotted a cotton-white flower, he leaned over to sniff the pleasant aroma, which pervaded his nose. Suddenly... SPLOSH! He tipped over, head-first, into the cerulean river, sending small tsunamis towards the boat.

"Help!" he stuttered desperately, his black and white head bobbing up and down in the water like a buoy...

Carefully, Ratty bent down, and both of their small hands clasped together. However, the weight was too much for Ratty, and he went tumbling down, head over heels, into the water, the exact way his friend had...

THE FLARE
A story by Allie Ng

The hill fire was rigorous. Snapping, hissing, crunching, the flares cocooned the building in a deathly embrace. Hiss! The inferno licked the red bricks of the building teasingly as a baby's terrified wails pierced the night air.

" I WANT MY MUMMY! WHAA!" she sobbed.

Faint-hearted, Hash was rooted to the spot like a plant, his fur coat smothering him like the smoke above him. As the baby's sobs mixed with the blade smoke, he closed his eyes and remembered Amy's adorable dimples when she smiled. His mouth twitched into a smile. Tears welled in his eyes. His heartbeat slowed. I miss her sunshine smile every day, he thought.

"Amy, this one's for you," he declared before diving into the conflagration like an angry beast...

The red and yellow ribbons of hostile flares wrapped themselves around him: it was a tower of fumes, a loop of toxic gas, an opaque prison. Determined, he lowered his head and flattened the wall of flames like a bulldozer.

Following the screams, Flash yelled, "Get as far as you can from the smoke and fumes! I'm nearly there with you."

He barged and tenderly scooped up the little baby girl from her pink cot - she leaned her head on his shoulder in relief.

Click clack! Flash's hurried footsteps matched his beating heart. His blonde hair was full of ash and his skin was even paler than usual. Fiercely, the fresh air blasted their faces as they stepped out of the building. Flash handed the baby to a pair of grateful parents before collapsing on the ground. She smiled her adorable dimples and reached for his hand.

"Amy?" he whispered before closing his eyes forever...

Tales of Adventure and Peril

THE WIND IN THE WILLOWS
A continuation by Alisa Alla

Scrambling and bustling, smiling and giggling, Mole continued his pursuit of life in the sun and air while excitement bubbled inside him. The sun - strong and vibrant - shone down like a spotlight. Mole was running when he spotted a shimmery apple tree.

"Hang spring-cleaning!" he said.

Suddenly, there was a... splash!

Behind him was now a wet Water Rat!

"Sorry!" exclaimed Mole "I really didn't mean to push you into the water."

"It's absolutely fine, after all I am a Water Rat," he explained.

Mole pulled Rat out of the river and hopped onto the boat.

"May I have a go on the skulls?" Mole questioned his new friend.

"Umm, maybe leave that part to me, okay?" Rat quickly answered.

"Okay," replied Mole, who was as excited as an athlete who just won a gold medal.

Relaxing, he shouted at the top of his lungs, "This truly is better than whitewashing!"

A few minutes later they came to a stop...

"Oh, my goodness!" they said in unison.

On the riverbanks was a wounded, terrified and agonised deer - it was bleeding! However, the flow of the river was too

KidzInk

rapid, and it took their boat, so neither Mole nor Rat could help, or at least know what pain the poor thing had suffered. This changed everything.

Suddenly, everything was quiet with not a single tweet to be heard...

THE OLD SMOKE
A descriptive piece by Aanya Shah

Like grinning angels, the lights of the city turned on to conceal the gloomy weather. Ancient buildings stand loftily, depicting opulence and grandeur while the atmosphere is an energetic party with enthusiasm exploding everywhere. Excitement whizzes through my skin. Beep! Beep! People honk their horns.

Despite the freezing weather taking over the sky, commuters proceed on their journey to work. The towering cathedral gazes down at the city while the thick, rancid smell of warm petrol and running engines dominates the air, catching the back of my throat.

Clip-clop! High heels stab the innocent ground; their noise competes with drivers venting their frustration. Even though it is a dull, dark, damp day, kids are still chatting like parakeets as the sun rises higher and displays a vivid ombre of pink and orange.

Splash! Light rain starts to drizzle down onto the jagged pavement - people gasp and then dart into nearby stores, creating a swarm inside. The shops are heaving! Watching the chaotic crowd gather into a quaint, mouth-watering bakery makes my stomach rumble as I inhale the aroma of freshly baked waffles coming out of the oven. The scent wafts up my nose.

Eventually, we carry on our journey, but out of nowhere, an annoying pigeon descends right outside our car, causing us to have to slam the brakes! Finally, the deafening sound dissipates, and cars in front of us start to crawl on. I turn the steering wheel and continue on my journey...

THE WIND IN THE WILLOWS
A continuation by Anaya Hussain

S campering and scuttling, smiling and beaming, Mole was continuing his pursuit of life in the sun and air when he spotted a pond. The little creature - curious and interested - noticed a Rat sitting at the edge of a lake.

"Oh, who is that?" he said as soft breezes caressed his heated brow.

Mole was inching closer when he realised the Rat - as panicked as a student before a test - wasn't sitting on the edge... He had fallen in...SPLASH!

Jumping off all his four legs, Mole was lightning itself to go and save him.

"Are you okay?" Mole asked.

"Yes," Rat replied while water dripped down him like a waterfall.

"Let me go and fetch you a towel from my home," the Mole stated.

"Okay, thank you," replied Ratty.

Mole rushed to his burrow, pushed the stubborn door in, and grabbed a clean towel before heading back to Rat.

"Here," said Mole, "I got you my favourite, brown, spotty towel", he said before catching his breath.

"Thank you so much," replied Ratty while Mole started to dry him.

A friendship had begun...

THIS IS THE CITY

A descriptive piece by Ella Walder

I breathe in and smell fresh raindrops. The water cleans the pavements while the aroma of pollution lingers in the autumn air. People brush past me, bustling and busy, despite the city showers.

Hostile air is a cold slap across the face. Beep! Honk! Blare! Cars toot their horns as high heels clip-clop on the pavement, like horses. Crimson buses are ladybirds scuttling around. I look up and see coin-grey clouds, looking, glaring, staring at the Big Smoke. A warm, welcoming scent hits me as pancakes are made, sizzled, and served...

Scarlet-red, marmalade-orange and parakeet-green traffic lights are the city's long-standing organisers. One man picks up a dropped wallet while another hurries into a shop; people are everywhere! The stench of pollution returns as a tiny peacock-blue car trundles past. I cough. Pelting rain starts falling yet again, however, this time mixed with the cold air, it feels like knives digging into my skin.

Within minutes, coin-grey clouds transform into hurrying, rumbling, evil puffs and the knives continue to sting. Above me, the cathedral stands his ground, his butterfly-blue dome unhurt by the blades of sharpness. I marvel at his grit. The clock chimes. The show started 5 minutes ago! I run towards the theatre, and away from it all.

This is the city.

THE WIND IN THE WILLOWS
A continuation by Avina Sohal

S cootering and scampering, smiling and beaming, Mole continued his pursuit of life in the sweltering sun and arid air while he hummed a majestic and meaningful melody. The little creature - who was as eager and excited as a toddler - went to explore. "This is so much more interesting than white-washing!" he exclaimed as he skipped under the pearlescent, puffy, and powder-white clouds.

Just then, Mole jumped off his four legs all at once, like a demented frog, because he heard an unknown voice say, "Hi fellow Mole, would you want to join me on my boat trip, as without your entertainment I would be melancholy and woebegone?"

In the blink of an eye, Mole curiously turned around and saw a slate-grey Water Rat whose name was Ratty.

"Hello, Ratty. Since you asked me so nicely, of course, it would be a pleasure to join you," explained Mole, who was bubbling with delight.

A few minutes after he boarded the boat, he felt that he should have the skulls as they were calling his name imperiously.

Pleadingly, he said, "Please may I steer the boat as I really want to?" Ratty replied worriedly, "Yes, you may, but be circumspect, cautious and careful as I made a mistake a few years ago and still have an injured toe due to that fateful error!"

Tales of Adventure and Peril

Without a second thought, Mole grabbed the skulls from Ratty's welcoming paws; all around him, the lake - which was reflective like a mirror - rippled in the blowing breeze.

"You are doing well, aren't you?" remarked Ratty. "Yes, I suppose I am," answered Mole with pride. However, Ratty had spoken too soon...

After half an hour or so, the sky brewed a storm and transformed into a monster. Sashes and swirls of hard wind blew down to the earth. The mindless Mole became over-confident and leaned back on the boat, falling off it before trying to save himself by clasping onto the rim of the boat with the tips of his fingers.

Splish, splash, splosh!

The deep, dark, and deadly lake, which was an open mouth, and tried to engulf him and whoever else came in its way, but it would not succeed... because the legend and hero, Ratty, hauled the poor thing up and Mole was saved!

Like a responsible older brother, Ratty scolded Mole by saying, rightfully, "Next time I will have the skulls. Now, as your glossy black fur is soaking wet, I will take you to my house and get you dried-up, and then we will enjoy some jam sandwiches and tea together!" "Thank you Ratty, I'm very grateful, and I will be for a lifetime; I appreciate that you are going to take me to your house and thank you for forgiving me, you are one in a million," said Mole with happy tears brimming in his eyes...

A STORMY SLIP AWAY
A Story by Misha Wong

C orn scanned the quiet classroom with a relaxed demeanour: the silence was as comforting as a fluffy blanket while the tidy rows of desks and polished floors were a reassurance to his eyes.

His face soon face scowled at the sight of the clock's hands sprinting towards eight o'clock, the start of the school day. Outside, the sun hid behind the elephant-grey clouds as a strong wind threatened to destroy the world - it was a glorious day for a storm.

"Noooo!" squeaked Corn when the clock's hour hand hit the number eight.

His furry, golden-brown body shivered as he waited for the bell to ring. However, the sound never came. Corn's brow furrowed, confused. It wasn't the weekend, nor was it a public holiday - why wasn't school starting?

He continued to sit quietly in his cage and stare at the clock: 8 o'clock. 9 o'clock. 10 o'clock. Still, no-one entered the classroom. By that point, Corn had finished the last of his hamster food and was starving. His mind drifted to the last time he was left alone without food...

Miss Denger – aka Miss Danger - his editor (Corn was one of those hamsters who wrote books) had ordered Corn to write ten chapters of his book before leaving for a party with her publisher. Reluctantly, he had finished the task but soon realised that she had not left any dinner for him. Corn was starved for eight consecutive hours and had almost fainted – he did not want the same thing to happen again!

A noisy rumble brought the little furry creature back to the present moment. He looked out the window: pitch-black clouds hung overhead while lashing rain drummed heavily everywhere. Thunder roared as if it were a confined animal, and blinding lightning struck every minute. Corn, terrified, sprinted to his sleeping corner and hid under the bedding. Soon, he was distracted by another rumble - not thunder, but a different one – his stomach!

"Oh no!" exclaimed Corn, starving. "I'm surely going to faint soon..." he announced dramatically to... nobody.

Refusing to give in, the golden hamster decided to get down to business and forage some food. He looked around. The only way to get out of his cage was through the locked door. All at once, Corn's face brightened like a lightbulb. Picking up his water bottle, he rammed it at the cage door. One... two... three! The door swung open! Corn rushed out of his cage, sweating like a marathon runner. Salivating, he scurried over to the food jars and dove into a pile of freeze-dried berries.

"Mmm," he murmured, chewing enthusiastically.

When he was finally full, he stood up and looked around. *I can either return to the safety of my cage, or escape through the window and risk the storm, not to mention potentially being destroyed by those big-wheeled monsters,* Corn thought. Gauging the situation, he decided to... risk it!

"I'm going on an adventure, everyone. Goodbye!" he shouted to the empty classroom, the empty cage, and the empty school.

KidzInk

Outside, a blast of wind nearly blew all of Corn's fur off. As the freezing rain pattered on him, he scurried down a red-brick wall onto the cold, hard, unyielding pavement. Seeking shelter, he buried himself under a rock.

"Oh, I actually hate this! Maybe this was a mistake after all," sighed Corn.

He was so busy thinking about his troubles that he failed to notice a shadow looming over him...

"Mum, what's that?" a little golden-haired boy asked. "Is it a hamster?"

"You're right, Oliver, that looks like an abandoned hamster," replied the woman with a kind face. "I wonder how that poor little thing got here..."

"Mum, please can we keep him? He's so cute and fluffy!" pleaded the boy. "I'll name him Corn because his fur is yellow!"

"Well... I suppose that could work," Oliver's mum sighed.

As Corn listened to the pair discussing his future, he knew he was going to have a new and happy life.

THE WIND IN THE WILLOWS
A continuation by Ayushi Thanabalan

Scampering and scuttling, smiling and giggling, Mole continued his pursuit of the stream while he took a glimpse here and there of the wildlife. The curious creature – excited and elated – skipped through the warm meadow. The grass – which was as soft as velvet – was jewelled with dew.

"This is actually quiet relaxing," he said sounding surprised.

"Help!" called a muffled voice.

"Hello?" Mole asked.

He looked into the sky-blue stream to see a Toad flailing his arms and panicking. Using all of his strength, Mole lunged into the water and grab hold of the poor thing. Splash!

"O, bother!" Mole and Toad said in an annoyed tone.

All at once, Mole tried to climb the rocks surrounding them, but he kept slipping and sliding: it was covered in limescale and moss. Cumbersome and awkward, their combined weight was too much to push themselves up.

Suddenly, Mole spotted a strange figure, and that same strange figure said in a muffled voice, "My name is Rat... hold onto my skulls, alright?"

Rat slowly lowered his skulls for Mole and Toad to climb onto.

"Thank you, Rat for helping us," Mole and Toad said as they climbed into his small, reddish-brown, wooden boat.

THE FURIOUS FIRE ALARM
A memoir by Jason Xu

The memory of that panic-inducing, alarming, terrorising day is as vivid as a flowerbed teeming with terrific tulips.

It all started when I was on a class trip at PGL. It was a picturesque day: the butter-yellow sun smiled down, and the sky was as clear as a newly polished window. I was on cloud nine. Resting on my bunk bed on my first night, I slowly drifted off to sleep...

After a few hours, I woke to a shrill screech. At first, I was bleary-eyed and clueless, thinking it was my group's door alarm (our lock was broken). Like a bulldozer, the realisation hit me: it was the fire alarm! I was rooted to the spot like an old tree. Fear grabbed at my throat. Bang! My friend leapt off the top bunk and landed on the floor, so I sprinted towards the exit and into the meeting place.

Outside, students and teachers were shaking and shivering. Some were crying for possessions while others were sobbing in fear. Meanwhile, I was still half asleep and trying to ward off an unforgiving cold. Fear grasped at me with its vice-like grip; anxiety coursed through my veins; nausea swirled in my stomach. Was there really a fire? Would we be okay? Would the rest of the trip go ahead as planned?

A few minutes later, our teachers did a head count; the piercing alarm was – to my relief – turned off. After all that, it turned out that somebody from a different school had used deodorant near the alarm, which had gone off as a result!

Tales of Adventure and Peril

Can you imagine? Something so small caused something so big. My heart soared as I felt the anxiety leave me, like an unwelcome guest going home.

After that day, I realised that sometimes things might seem scary, but they're not as serious as all that. It's best to expect the unexpected but to also think positive!

THE WIND IN THE WILLOWS
A continuation by Aaral Bhandari

Scurrying and skipping, smiling, and singing, Mole was enjoying the delight of spring, a spring that was moving in the air! Soft breezes caressed his heated brow. The grass - sweet and lush - glittered in the scorching sun, while the lake - mesmerising as a crystal-blue fire – shimmered and glimmered in delight.

"This is better than whitewashing!" exclaimed Mole, full of joy.

Excitement bubbled inside him with every step, but little did he know his peace and excitement would be short-lived.

Hearing a faint noise, Mole felt alarmed. From the corner of his eye, he sensed a pair of bright, bronzy, brown eyes boring into him. Instantly, jumping off all his four legs at once, he decided to gingerly make his way towards a hiding spot where he noticed a sharp shadow stalking him - it was the cruel, cunning owl trying to gobble Mole for lunch...!

In the very next moment, a miracle happened: he found himself under the warm leaves of the meadow.

"Thank goodness, I am saved!" he reassured himself.

However, once again, little did Mole know that he was stuck in a trap set by vicious hunters. He scraped and scratched and scrabbled and Scrooged but with no luck. Every effort went in vain.

"O, bother, O' blow!" Mole said in a panic as each muscle tensed, and sweat poured from his body.

Without a single second wasted, he yelled and pleaded until he caught Rat's attention.

"My, my! What has happened to you Mole?" enquired Rat.

Mole - shivering and stuttering - replied, "My dear friend, will you please help me from this terrible, torturous trap?"

Hurriedly, Rat sprang into action; rat nibbled the mesh with his razor-sharp teeth and made a hole wide enough for Mole to rescue...

Pop! Mole was free.

TRAPPED

A story by Yu Wong

S awyer took in the field with excitement: the laughter was as loud as the crowd during the Olympics while the children's smiles were as joyous as Christmas. Everyone's faces lit up at the sight of the football swishing into the net. Above them, the sun - high up in the sky - beamed at the youngsters. It was a wondrous day!

An hour later, Sawyer arrived home, his initial joyous mood instantly changing into one of depression. The reason? His father was greeting him at the door with a shiny smile.

"Hey Sawyer!" You're back!" he exclaimed. "How was school?"

"Hey, Dad. Um... it was..." he bit his tongue hard to stop himself from saying, "better than at home,". "It was good!" A salty, metallic taste filled his mouth.

"That's good!" his father replied. "Oh, I forgot to tell you that we are both on night shift tonight, so remember to finish your homework. I'll be checking when I get in!"

Finally, Sawyer thought, *I can have some free time to myself!*

It was the first time in years that both his parents had a night shift on the same evening, so he couldn't wait for them to leave; within two hours, they were at the door.

"Bye, Sawyer! Remember to finish your homework! Work must always come first!" his parents cried in unison.

"Okay, I will. Bye, Mum! Bye, Dad!" Sawyer replied.

Once the door was closed, Sawyer shouted, "Yes!" while immediately taking a tub of ice-cream from the fridge, turning on the tv, and generally having fun.

However, his fun came to an abrupt end when he glanced out of the window and saw two men in balaclavas, standing behind a tree, peering into the house.

"Thieves? Oh no!" Sawyer started to think as he erratically tidied up his mess. He was soon ready for the thieves to make the biggest mistake of their lives...

First, he found all his parents' valuables and brought them into his room, hoping that the burglars would steer clear of a child's room. Next, he took a suitcase from his parents' bedroom and stuffed it full of his homework (for the entire month!) Finally, he turned off the light and went to sleep, hoping his plan would work like a dream...

The next morning, Sawyer woke up with the sun at 5am and ran around his room. Valuables? Check! Homework? He would have to go into his parents' room to check.

Tiptoeing in with trepidation, he walked in and looked everywhere – the suitcase with all his homework in was gone! The valuables were safe, and he wouldn't have to do homework for an entire month!

With joy, he gobbled his breakfast, ready to go to school.

THE FLARE

A story by Aarya Kotecha

The remorseless inferno was nefarious. Sweltering, searing, sizzling, the sea of flames embraced the building. Crash! A brick fell to the ground as a seven-year-old, blonde-haired girl screamed from the top of the building.

"Help! I need help!" she vociferated, "I can't get down, and I'm going to melt!"

Paralysed, Asher was glued to the ground, his fire extinguisher lying patiently by his feet. As his father's last words to him replayed in his mind for the millionth time, he closed his eyes and remembered his warm smile. His mouth twitched. His eyes were filled with puddles of water. His heartbeat slowed. *I wish he could be here now, he thought.*

"This is for Dad," he whispered passionately before rushing into the flames like Icarus flying towards the sun...

Forcefully, heat hit him, knocking him for six: it was a suffocating stranglehold, a noose of noxious gas, a poisonous prison. Determined, Asher lunged at the wall of fumes and tore through it...

Following the cries like ambulance sirens, he yelled, 'Don't panic! I'm almost there!" he soothed, trying to feel for the girl, like a blind man trying to feel his way in the world, through the black smoke. When he found Emme, she buried her charcoal-covered face in Asher's coat.

"Come on," he said reassuringly, "let's go."

Like professional racers, they were sprinting through the building when the staircase gave way.

"How will we get out now?!" cried Emme, right when the windows shattered.

Glass flew everywhere, so Asher used his arm to shield him and Emme.

"Out of the window!" he replied.

He grabbed Emme's arm, and they both jumped out just as an enormous wave of fire engulfed the building.

When they were away from the depraved blaze, Emme thanked him, then hugged him like a father.

"Mummy!" the little girl squealed when she saw her mother.

She limped towards her as quickly as possible, considering her leg broke when jumping.

"Emme, thank goodness you're okay!" her mother sighed with relief.

Her father appeared, too, and he rushed to Emme.

"Thank you, Asher," they both said very appreciatively.

Asher was drinking water when they heard another voice. It was coming from the building. Realising his job wasn't done, he grabbed his pack and bravely strode into the flames once more...

KidzInk

ACKNOWLEDGEMENTS

To all the parents, your loyalty and support over the years is the only reason I can do a job I love. Thank you for, first, enrolling your child and, later, for scanning, printing, emailing, and repeatedly choosing me to be your child's creative writing teacher over all the tutors out there – I hope that perilous decision led to adventure!

A huge thank you to Bill McConkey, the Master of the Illo Universe, for designing two gorgeous covers for KidzInk out of the goodness and passion of his heart. You created the cover of dreams with this one, which instantly elevated the entire project. No-one does it better. We owe you!

To my first and best friend, Eva, for listening to my stories for 38 years. To my mum, who still thinks I teach children the alphabet, but who is my most fervent champion. To my dad, whose stories of eating pomegranates in Cyprus always make me smile. To my brother, Costas, who was the only person to encourage me to quit my day job – sometimes you need someone who has already been on the journey to say it's worth it.

To my sweet niece Maya, who is so curious about the stories of the world, and whose laugh is my favourite sound in the world.

To Nick de Semlyen, my favourite person to adventure with, who has taught me so much about words and stories, who has made my life much bigger and brighter by virtue of being in it, and who has shown me the importance of honouring everything I do with care and attention (although some typos will live on forever). Thank you for never tiring of pretending to be a nine-year-old so I can practise my lessons on you, and for all of it.

Finally, to all the children who have attended KidzInk over the years, from 2017 to the present day. Thank you for coming to all my makeshift classrooms around North London – from the noisy cafés to the dusty but cosy libraries, we found a way to keep writing stories. Thank you for sticking with me when I moved to video teaching – such a scary and unknown concept back then – and for racing back from school, scoffing something quick to eat, and working for an extra hour and a half at the end of a long day. Thank you for telling me about the books you're reading, and your sweet and fun lives. You are always at the heart of what I do, and the KidzInk community would not exist without you. Just remember to unmute - on Zoom, and in life.

We read and write on!

Printed in Great Britain
by Amazon